Dear
Police Officer
We Thank You

Daphnee Salomon

AuthorHouse™
1663 Liberty Drive
Bloomington, IN 47403
www.authorhouse.com
Phone: 833-262-8899

Because of the dynamic nature of the Internet, any web addresses or links contained in this book may have changed since publication and may no longer be valid. The views expressed in this work are solely those of the author and do not necessarily reflect the views of the publisher, and the publisher hereby disclaims any responsibility for them.

Any people depicted in stock imagery provided by Getty Images are models, and such images are being used for illustrative purposes only. Certain stock imagery © Getty Images.

This book is printed on acid-free paper.

ISBN: 978-1-6655-2719-4 (sc)
978-1-6655-2718-7 (e)

Library of Congress Control Number: 2021910642

Print information available on the last page.

Published by AuthorHouse 05/24/2021

authorHOUSE®

Dear
Police Officer
We Thank You

Dear Police Officer,
we thank you!

A police officer has a very important job. He/She protects and serves everybody!

Their duties are various and valuable.

They help you cross the street.

They give tickets to the people driving too fast so you don't get hurt when walking outside. So you can help too by following the speed limit.

They chase, catch and put the bad guys in jail.

They patrol the streets at night to make sure you sleep safe.

When you're in trouble just dial 911, and a police officer will run to your rescue!

All we do in return is show respect and love to let them know how much we appreciate their great service.

Thank you Mr. Police Officer for everything you do!

Printed in the United States
by Baker & Taylor Publisher Services